BINH VO

THE BOY WHO INSPIRED SANTA

NICK

illusgtrated by HOAI NAM

GRIT AND GLORY:
AGAINST-ALL-ODDS STORIES OF FAMOUS FIGURE SERIES

EINSTEIN: The Boy Who Changed the World (3.2023)

THE TRUNG SISTERS: The Girls Who Defied An Empire
(8.2023)

SCAN TO ORDER

EINSTEIN:
THE BOY WHO CHANGED THE WORLD

SCAN TO ORDER

THE TRUNG SISTERS:
THE GIRLS WHO DEFIED AN EMPIRE

For Asher, whose smile illuminates my days,
May your life be filled with joy and grace.

Is Santa Real?

"Nick: The Boy Who Inspired Santa" celebrates the historical Saint Nicholas. He was a real person whose kindness inspired the magical stories of Santa Claus. Saint Nicholas lived a long time ago—around 1,700 years ago—in a place that's part of modern-day Turkey, in a town called Myra.

One famous story tells of how Nick helped three sisters who needed a dowry, which is money given to help someone start a new life when they get married. These sisters didn't have a dowry, but Nick came up with a clever plan to help them without anyone knowing it was him. This was really important because it allowed the sisters to not feel embarrassed. He quietly dropped bags of gold down their chimney, and one bag happened to fall into a stocking that was hung to dry. This could be one of the reasons we have the tradition of filling stockings at Christmas!

In many ways, Nick was like the Santa Claus we think of today. The kind Saint Nicholas from long ago started the tradition of giving gifts that led to the Santa tales we know and love. All around the world, people tell different stories about Santa, but what matters most is the giving and kindness he represents. The happiness we share through giving is the real magic of Christmas. This is a truth that belongs to everyone, everywhere.

For parents:

Introducing "Find Nick's Coins," an interactive experience that accompanies our story "Nick - The Boy Who Inspired Santa." This activity encourages children to use their detective skills, celebrate the spirit of giving, and practice counting as they keep track of the coins they've uncovered.

Can you help find all the golden coins that Nick has left behind?

As you read the story, look for shiny golden coins hidden throughout the book. There are 12 coins waiting to be found. Can you find all 12 coins? Remember to celebrate each time you find a coin!

Here's a hint:

The coins look similar to the one in the image below. Happy hunting!

Copyright © 2023 Binh Vo. Illustrations copyright © 2023 Binh Vo. All rights reserved. No part of this book may be reproduced or transmitted in any form or by any means, electronic or mechanical, including photocopying, recording, or by any information storage and retrieval system, without written permission from the author.

ISBN: 9798867170806

Emotikids
BOOKS

In a land by the Mediterranean Sea,
Lived a young boy named Nick, who was kind as can be.

From wealthy parents, he learned love and grace,
That true joy comes from the kindness we embrace.

But a shadow cast over their bright, sunny days,
A plague came to town, leaving darkness in its haze.

Nick's parents fought bravely, yet were taken away,
Leaving young Nick all alone to find his own way.

As he wandered the streets, what he began to see,
Were glimpses of pain, a vast sea of misery.

He saw young orphans, lost without a home,
No safe haven, through the streets they would roam.

"My grief is but one drop in this vast teary sea,"
"There's much I can do with the wealth given to me."

Each silent night, as he shed countless tears,
His father's wise words echoed in his ears.

His father once said, "Joy's not just receiving,"
"True happiness grows with selfless, heartfelt giving."

Nick's mission was clear, his path now defined,
To bring happiness to all of mankind.

He sold his treasures, his silver and gold,
Gave to the needy, the young, and the old.

As he grew, so did his acts of goodwill,
Coins left in shoes, toys on windowsills.

Cloaked, Nick vanished into the silent night,
Gifting in secret, avoiding the limelight.

One night, Nick heard a father's heartfelt plea,
For three dowries to set his daughters free.

Three daughters he had, with no dowries to wed,
A life of despair and hardship lay ahead.

Under the cover of the starlit night,
Nick climbed the chimney with gold shining bright.

He lowered the bags beneath the night sky,
Into stockings hung by the fireside.

Morning came, the sisters cheered in surprise,
"Who was so kind?" they asked, tears in their eyes.

This inspired the people to fill stockings with care,
With gifts for their loved ones, spreading joy in the air.

Thus, the stocking tradition was born and held dear,
For children to await gifts on Christmas each year.

Nick grew up to be a man of kindness and love,
He became a bishop and served the Lord above.

His deeds turned to legends, his fame spread through the land,
As Saint Nick, he became known as the "giving hand."

Through ages and tales, his story's been spun,
From Saint Nick to Santa, they've become one.

Though stories have changed, one truth still remains,
The spirit of giving, in Saint Nick's name.

Christmas is not about the presents we receive,
But the spirit of giving in which we should believe.

Help those in need, make someone's troubles disappear,
Donate to charity, lend a listening ear.

A simple act can truly go a long way,
A long, warm hug can brighten anyone's day.

Assist an elder crossing the busy street,
And offer a warm smile to those you meet.

Take the time to do a kind deed today,
And weave these acts of love into each day.

Each act of kindness makes the season bright,
Merry Christmas to all, and to all a good night.

Made in the USA
Middletown, DE
24 November 2024

65317685R00018